FREEDOM FORCES

★ U.S. NAVY: ★
NAVAL POWER

Tom Greve

Rourke
Educational Media
rourkeeducationalmedia.com

© 2014 Rourke Educational Media LLC

J359
GRE

www.rourkeeducationalmedia.com

PHOTO CREDITS: Cover photo © Lockheed Martin, metal border © Molodec; back cover photo and title page photo © Iakov Kalinin, back cover and title page flag © SFerdon, back cover metal border © Molodec; Pages 4/5 © US Navy, U.S. Navy National Museum of Naval Aviation; Pages 6/7 © Marc Sitkin, Orionist; Pages 8/9 © NPS.gov, Rear Admiral John William Schmidt, Mass Communication Specialist 2nd Class Matthew D. Williams, US Navy; Pages 10/11 © Mass Communication Specialist 1st Class Chad J. McNeeley, US Navy, Hunter Stires; Pages 12/13 © Scott A. Thornbloom, US Navy Pages 14/15 © Photographer's Mate Airman Rob Gaston, US Navy, Mass Communication Specialist 1st Class James R. Evans; Pages 16/17 © Mass Communication Specialist 2nd Class Zane Ecklund US Navy, Photographer's Mate 3rd Class John DeCoursey US Navy; Pages 18/19 © US Navy, Photographer's Mate 3rd Class Summer M. Anderson US Navy; Pages 20/21 © Bob Kopprasch, Mass Communication Specialist 1st Class James R. Evans US Navy; Pages 22/23 © Mass Communication Specialist 3rd Class Billy Ho US Navy, Chief Mass Communication Specialist John Lill US Navy, Photographer's Mate 2nd Class Jayme Pastoric US Navy, Photographer's Mate 1st Class Michael W. Pendergrass US Navy, Petty Officer 1st Class James R. Evans U.S. Navy, Chief Mass Communication Specialist Jennifer L. Walker US Navy, Jerry Gunner, Mass Communication Specialist 3rd Class Kenneth Abbate US Navy, Mass Communication Specialist 1st Class John M. Hageman US Navy Pages 24/25 © National Archives and Records Administration, IndianSummer; Pages 26/27 © Michael Foran, Chief Photographer's Mate Eric J. Tllford, FBI; Pages 28/29 © NPS.gov, Charles Robert Patterson, US Navy, National Archives and Records Administration, TastyCakes

Edited by Precious McKenzie

Designed and Produced by Blue Door Publishing, FL

Library of Congress Cataloging-in-Publication Data

Greve. Tom
 U.S. Navy: Naval Power / Tom Greve
 p. cm. -- (Freedom Forces)
 ISBN 978-1-62169-923-1 (hard cover) (alk. paper)
 ISBN 978-1-62169-818-0 (soft cover)
 ISBN 978-1-62717-027-7 (e-book)
Library of Congress Control Number: 2013938875

Also Available as:
ROURKE'S
e-Books

Rourke Educational Media
Printed in the United States of America,
North Mankato, Minnesota

Rourke
Educational Media

rourkeeducationalmedia.com
customerservice@rourkeeducationalmedia.com
PO Box 643328 Vero Beach, Florida 32964

TABLE OF CONTENTS

The U.S. Navy has a long history of defending the nation from threats at sea. The Navy's success in World War II altered the course of history in favor of the United States.

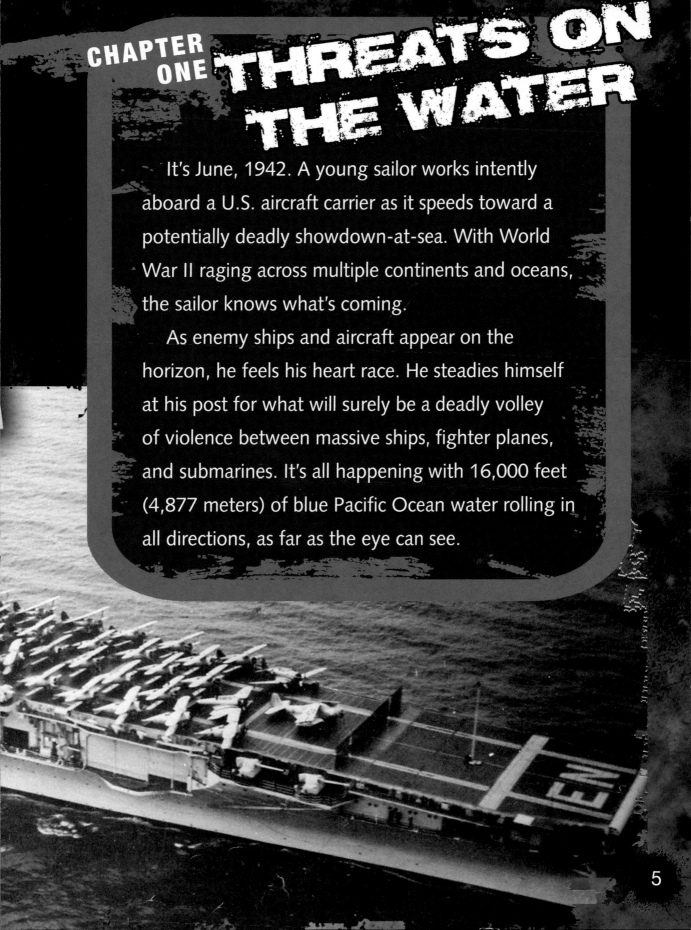

CHAPTER ONE THREATS ON THE WATER

It's June, 1942. A young sailor works intently aboard a U.S. aircraft carrier as it speeds toward a potentially deadly showdown-at-sea. With World War II raging across multiple continents and oceans, the sailor knows what's coming.

As enemy ships and aircraft appear on the horizon, he feels his heart race. He steadies himself at his post for what will surely be a deadly volley of violence between massive ships, fighter planes, and submarines. It's all happening with 16,000 feet (4,877 meters) of blue Pacific Ocean water rolling in all directions, as far as the eye can see.

The U.S. Navy is the nation's combat and security force of the high seas. It might be hard to tell by just looking around, but we live in a world of water. In fact, oceans cover 70 percent of planet Earth's surface, leaving about seven billion human beings to live on dry land.

The ocean is much more than a watery expanse between the continents. It is also a highway, a food source, and a battlefield.

ARCTIC OCEAN

UNITED STATES

ATLANTIC OCEAN

PACIFIC OCEAN

INDIAN OCEAN

PACIFIC OCEAN

SOUTHERN OCEAN

There are more than 40 naval bases here in the United States, with others situated around the world.

The United States is a **superpower** with the world's largest military force. The Navy, along with the Army, Air Force, and Marines, all play roles in defending the country against forces that would aim to harm the nation, its people, or its resources.

CHAPTER TWO

U.S. NAVAL HISTORY

The U.S. Navy dates back to the Revolutionary War and the Continental Navy. Even while under British rule, the American colonies identified the need to have a defense force operating in the Atlantic Ocean. So in 1775, as the colonies began their fight to gain independence from Great Britain, colonial leaders formed the Continental Navy.

Notable Naval Hero:
The Continental Navy quickly grew its fleet of ships and its ranks of sailors. Among them was John Paul Jones, considered the nation's first naval hero. Jones successfully commanded several revolutionary warships. He launched sea attacks on British ships and even sailed across the Atlantic Ocean to attack British ports.

John Paul Jones
1747-1792

The Continental Navy started with just a few merchant ships outfitted with weapons and a group of merchant sailors trying to disable British ships bringing supplies to the British Army.

By 1785, the U.S. had secured victory against Great Britain. With no pressing threat looming in the Atlantic Ocean, and in need of money to set up an effective federal government, the newly-elected Congress sold the Continental Navy's ships. However, the United States' constitution, ratified just four years later in 1789, called for Congress to create and maintain a national navy.

By 1794, Congress ordered the construction of six ships and crews of sailors to operate the ships. From this humble beginning arose a naval force that today consists of nearly 300 vessels, including nuclear-powered submarines, aircraft carriers, and more than 3,000 aircraft.

The U.S. Navy has grown throughout history both in terms of sailors and ships. At the forefront of **maritime** technology, the Navy's fleet of ships has become bigger, faster, and more efficient in responding to threats over the past 240 years.

The technology of modern navy ships has little in common with the USS Constitution. In fact, the Navy's fleet has grown to include not just massive combat ships, but submarines, and airplanes as well.

The U.S. Navy, like all of the U.S. military branches, operates under the overall command of the elected President of the United States. That is why the President also carries the title Commander-in-Chief.

Old Ironsides

The USS Constitution *was one of the U.S. Navy's original tall sail ships. Named by none other than George Washington. The ship had protective copper plating to protect its hull from rot, and a tight design for hauling cannons. It became an important part of U.S. Naval strategy through the first half of the 1800s. The ship, affectionately known as Old Ironsides, is still afloat. It serves as a Naval Museum at its port in Boston, Massachusetts.*

CHAPTER THREE

THE SAILORS:
HONOR, COURAGE, COMMITMENT

Active duty members of the U.S. Navy are sailors. This term harkens back to the earliest days of the Navy when its **vessels** were sailing ships. Currently, there are more than 300,000 active duty sailors serving in the U.S. Navy and more than 50,000 in the Navy Reserves, making it the largest navy on Earth.

Every Navy recruit goes through basic training, or boot camp, at the Great Lakes Naval Base in Illinois. Navy recruits have to be at least 17 years old and go through eight weeks of physical fitness and training drills to begin living by the Navy's motto: Honor, Courage, and Commitment.

A modern Navy ship is like a floating city, with hundreds and even thousands of sailors working on board at any time. Each sailor performs a specific job in the overall operation and maintenance of the ship and everything on it. Some are radar operators or computer technicians, some work preparing food, some work on maintenance crews. Sailors also drill for readiness in case of combat.

Women In The Navy

Females have been serving in the U.S. Navy since 1908. Although they began serving as nurses, they have expanded their role to include virtually every post in the modern Navy. There are now female officers and there have been female ship commanders. As of 2013, women can even serve in combat positions. Overall, women make up about 18 percent of the Navy's total personnel.

Female Navy Personnel

Male Navy Personnel

The vast majority of people who join the U.S. Navy will spend time at sea. For most, that means on a ship. For others, it might be on a submarine. Either way, life at sea means long days, tight spaces, and strictly following Navy rules and training.

Instead of rooms for sleeping, sailors sleep in bunks stacked on top of one another almost like dresser drawers. Personal items go in an upright locker, or in compartments under the bunk.

Sailors at sea have to be able to live in close proximity to one another. Space on a ship is valuable and limited. Space is even more limited on a nuclear submarine where the specially trained crew goes about their work for up to six months at a time without ever seeing daylight.

Naval Service Commitment:
When a sailor joins the Navy, he or she commits to a certain length of service. Most active duty sailors sign on for an initial commitment of 4 years. For Navy Reservists, or part-time sailors, the commitment can be as little as two years. At the end of their commitment, they have the option to re-enlist.

Some of the Navy's nuclear-powered subs never need refueling. The only reason they ever need to surface and dock is to swap out crews or replenish food supplies.

The U.S. Navy is a complex group of sailors who bring a wide range of skills to bear not only in operating and maintaining the Navy's fleet, but also in defense of the country.

Draft vs. Volunteer:
From World War I through the Vietnam War, the U.S. used drafts to build up the military during wartime. That meant all young men were eligible for **mandatory** service in the country's armed forces. Since 1973 however, men and women volunteer to serve, including in the U.S. Navy and Reserves.

Highly skilled and physically fit sailors can test into elite Special Operation Command forces. These forces have grown in size and mission in recent years. The Army, Marines, and Air Force each have Special Operation Command units within their organization.

The Navy SEALs

The Navy boasts an especially skilled Special Operations Command force called the Navy SEALs. Candidates have to pass extremely tough physical entrance tests, and undergo a variety of specialized trainings. SEAL stands for Sea, Air, and Land, which represents their wide-ranging skill at attacking an enemy; in the sea, from the air, or on land.

CHAPTER FOUR

THE SHIPS

From the wooden sailing ships of the late 1700s to its modern fleet of aircraft carriers, warships, and submarines, the Navy's ability to project power from the sea comes in large part, from its vessels.

USS *Nimitz* is a floating powerhouse of sea-to-air combat readiness. It is among the world's largest warships, with a crew of roughly 6,000 sailors and aviation personnel. It can carry up to 90 aircraft on its deck.

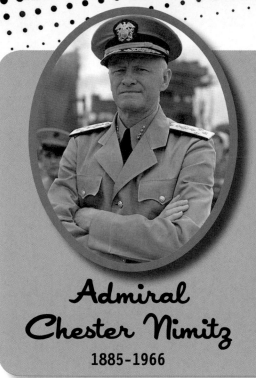

Notable Naval Hero:

The Navy's largest carriers are all categorized as Nimitz-class carriers. The classification is named in honor of Admiral Chester Nimitz, the top Naval Commander of World War II, and among the most decorated sailors in U.S. history. He is the last man to hold the title of Fleet Admiral of the U.S. Navy.

Admiral Chester Nimitz
1885-1966

The modern aircraft carrier was a military response to the increased use of airplanes in combat during World War I. Aircraft carriers are like floating airports that can navigate the ocean into position as an air attack base near a combat **theater**. The largest carriers use nuclear reactors for power.

The USS *George Washington* is another Nimitz-class carrier. It is nuclear-powered, and only needs to be refueled about once every 18 years.

The Navy and the U.S. Marine Corps often work in tandem. The Marines are a forward-operating amphibious combat force. This means they can attack an enemy from the sea and advance forward on land. The Navy provides Marines with transportation and **logistical** support at sea.

The USS *New York* is one of the Navy's amphibious warships. These vessels can unload marines and cargo directly onto land without the need of a pier, dock, or separate landing craft.

The Navy's latest combat ship design is a **littoral** combat ship. It is capable of open ocean maneuvers and combat, but it is built for use in waters of the littoral zone, or shallow shoreline areas of the sea.

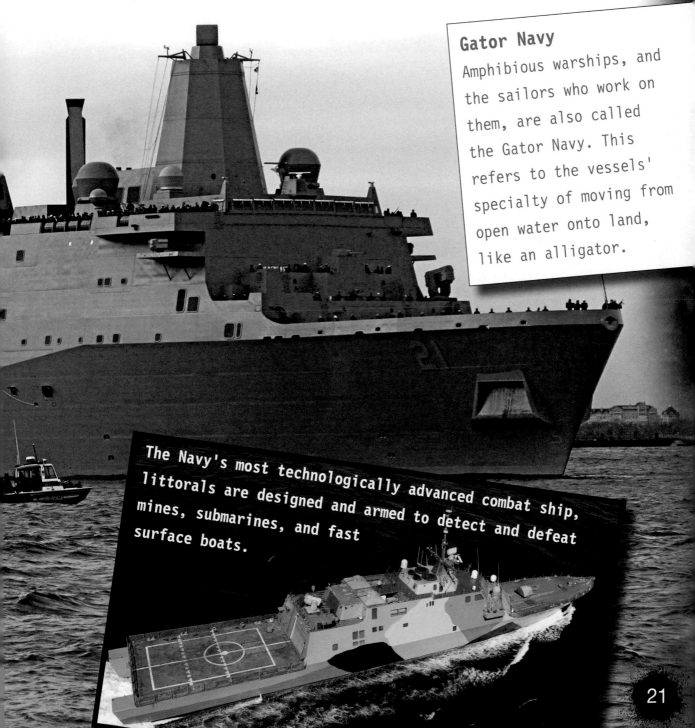

Gator Navy
Amphibious warships, and the sailors who work on them, are also called the Gator Navy. This refers to the vessels' specialty of moving from open water onto land, like an alligator.

The Navy's most technologically advanced combat ship, littorals are designed and armed to detect and defeat mines, submarines, and fast surface boats.

Main vessels and Aircraft of The U.S. Navy's Fleet:

Aircraft Carriers

Amphibious Assault Ships

Cruisers

Destroyers

Littoral Combat Ships

Frigates

Submarines

Fighter Jets

Helicopters

Stealth Submarines:

Serving as the Navy's hidden weapon beneath the waves, submarines are much smaller than ships, but can cross the ocean without ever coming to the surface. Submarines are highly technical and complex vessels, requiring specially trained crews. They can launch missiles capable of sinking an enemy ship without ever being detected.

CHAPTER FIVE

THE TRIUMPHS

Twice in the past century, the U.S. Navy has rallied in response to attacks on the U.S. homeland. The 1941 Japanese attack on Pearl Harbor, Hawaii, and the 2001 **terrorist** attack on New York City and Washington D.C. left the nation with a sense of outrage and violation.

ATTACK ON PEARL HARBOR!

On December 7th, 1941, hundreds of Japanese fighter planes bombed the U.S. Naval base at Pearl Harbor, Hawaii. Four U.S. battleships sank, and more than 2,000 Americans died in the surprise attack. The U.S. declared war on Japan the very next day, and the U.S. Navy began its largest response to an attack in history.

Following the attack, the U.S. Navy quickly regrouped and from early 1942 until 1945, battled the Japanese Navy throughout the Pacific Ocean. A series of battles and U.S. victories forced the action ever closer to the Japanese mainland.

Naval Triumph at Midway Island!

Thanks in part to U.S. Navy radio operators intercepting enemy messages, the U.S. Navy knew the Japanese planned to attack the U.S. airstrip on Midway Island. Using this information, the U.S. Navy launched an ambush of its own against the Japanese fleet, sinking four of Japan's ships. With the victory at Midway, the U.S. Navy turned the tide of World War II in the Pacific theater.

25

While the U.S. naval battles of World War II played out against conventional enemies, the attacks of September 11th were done by a secretive terrorist network known as al Qaeda. The U.S. military, including the Navy, has had to alter its combat approach in fighting these terrorist groups who use stealth, timing, and **guerrilla** tactics to attack, rather than using conventional forces like an army or a navy.

Terrorist Attacks of September 11th, 2001

Terrorist **hijackers** angry at U.S. military policy in parts of the Middle East took control of commercial airplanes and crashed them into places like New York City's World Trade Center and the Pentagon building in Washington D.C. Nearly 3,000 people died in the attack, most of them at the World Trade Center. The U.S. immediately began planning an invasion of Afghanistan where the suspected masterminds of the attacks were hiding.

The U.S. Navy has been in the Gulf of Oman and other parts of the Middle East since shortly after the attack. Unlike the ocean battles of World War II, the Navy has increasingly fought **insurgent** groups on shore. The Navy's littoral warships are part of the combat focus in the Navy's fight against terrorists since September 11, 2001, along with an increased role of Special Forces, and even the use of unmanned drone aircraft.

U.S. Navy SEALs insignia

Navy SEALs Kill Terrorist Leader

In May of 2011, the Navy's elite special forces combat unit known as SEAL Team 6 performed a daring midnight raid on the suspected Pakistan hideout of al Qaeda leader and September 11th attack mastermind Osama bin Laden. Operating with a surgeon's precision and overwhelming force, the SEALs killed bin Laden and captured evidence of other terrorist activities. It was a triumph a decade in the making, and a high point in what has become the longest military conflict in U.S. history.

Osama bin Laden 1957-2011

TIMELINE

1779:

John Paul Jones commands Continental Navy over British ship Serapis.

1797:

USS *Constitution*, Navy's first ironclad sailing warship.

1816:

USS *Fulton*, Navy's first steam-powered ship.

1922:

USS *Langley* converted into Navy's first aircraft carrier.

1939:

Navy researchers develop radar (Radio Detection and Ranging) for use on ships for navigation and enemy detection.

1941:

U.S. Fleet attacked by Japanese at Pearl Harbor, Hawaii, starting World War II.

1949:

Navy's first jet engine fighter plane — Grumman Panther.

1955:

Navy begins using nuclear energy to power submarines.

1975:

USS *Nimitz*, Navy's first nuclear-powered aircraft carrier.

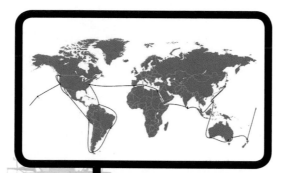

1900:
USS *Holland*, Navy's first submarine.

1904:
The Great White Fleet of U.S. Navy circumnavigates the globe.

1912:
Naval aviation begins- First landing of an airplane onto the deck of a ship in San Diego.

1942:
U.S. Navy defeats Japan in Battle of Midway.

1944:
Navy launches two ships with racially integrated crews. On board is Samuel Gravely, who would become the Navy's first African-American admiral.

1945:
Japan surrenders aboard the USS *Missouri*- ending World War II in the Pacific.

1990:
Lieutenant Commander Darlene Iskra becomes first female U.S. ship commander.

2001:
Navy responds to terror attack, Invasion of Afghanistan.

2011:
Navy SEALs locate and kill Osama bin Laden.

2013:
First unmanned fighter drone aircraft launched from Navy aircraft carrier.

SHOW WHAT YOU KNOW

1. When was the U.S. Navy founded?
2. What do we call the men and women who serve in the Navy?
3. Name the types of vessels the Navy uses.
4. Why is a Navy ship like a floating city?
5. What does the U.S. Navy do to protect the United States?

GLOSSARY

guerilla (guh-RIH-lah): combatants who hide and use surprise attacks against a larger military

hijackers (HYE-jak-erz): people who forcefully take over an airplane to change its destination

insurgent (in-SUR-juhnt): a person armed against an authority, government, or military

littoral (luh-TOR-uhl): the part of a body of water nearest the shore

logistical (lo-JIS-tik-uhl): having to do with the arrangement and movement of people and supplies on a schedule

mandatory (MAN-dih-TOR-ee): required, not optional

maritime (MA-ruh-time): having to do with ships, the sea, or navigation

superpower (SOO-per-POW-uhr): a nation with advanced economic and military power capable of shaping global politics

terrorist (TER-uhr-ist): a person who frightens society with violent acts in order to affect change

theater (THEE-uh-tur): a region where combat takes place

vessels (VESS-ulsz): ships, submarines, or large boats

Index

Websites to Visit

www.navy.mil

www.pacificwarmuseum.org

www.navyreserve.com

About the Author

Tom Greve lives in Chicago. He is married, has two children, and enjoys reading and writing about military history. He has an older brother who served six years in the U.S. Navy. He is grateful to all who have served in the U.S. Military.

Meet The Author!
www.meetREMauthors.com